Julius Bissier

1893-1965
A RETROSPECTIVE EXHIBITION

Messer, Thomas M.

LENDERS TO THE EXHIBITION

Sarah G. Austin, New York
Mrs. Robert M. Benjamin, New York
Mr. and Mrs. Jerome Brody, New York
Mrs. Andrew Fuller, New York
Mr. and Mrs. L. F. Gittler, New York
Mr. and Mrs. Richard Hofstadter, New York
Joseph H. Hirshhorn Collection, New York
Erhart and Anita Kästner, Wolfenbüttel
Mr. and Mrs. George Labalme, Jr., New York
John Lefebre, New York
Mrs. John Lefebre, New York
Marion Lefebre, New York
Mr. and Mrs. Gustave Levy, New York
Mrs. H. Gates Lloyd, Haverford, Pennsylvania
New England Merchants National Bank of Boston
Dr. Werner Schmalenbach, Düsseldorf
Mr. and Mrs. R. B. Schulhof, New York
Mr. and Mrs. Peter A. Silverman, Toronto
Mr. and Mrs. David Steine, Nashville

The Cleveland Museum of Art
Museum of Fine Arts, Boston
The Museum of Modern Art, New York
Staatliche Museen Preussischer Kulturbesitz,
    Nationalgalerie, Berlin
Staatsgalerie, Stuttgart
The Tate Gallery, London

Galerie Beyeler, Basel
Lefebre Gallery, New York

ACKNOWLEDGEMENTS   On behalf of the Board of Trustees of the San Francisco Museum of Art and the participating institutions, I want to express our warmest gratitude to the lenders to the exhibition and to Mrs. Lisbeth Bissier. Mrs. Bissier, the artist's widow, has made continuous efforts on behalf of the exhibition for well over a year. Her unflagging efforts in connection with Mr. Messer's research and my selection of works from the Bissier Estate and from her own collection have made the exhibition possible. Mrs. Bissier's devotion to her husband and his work has been a beautiful example to us all.

Special thanks are due to Dr. Werner Schmalenbach, Director of the Nordrhein-Westfalen Museum, Düsseldorf, for his advice on selection, for the use of his library, and for his loan to the exhibition. Dr. Schmalenbach's name is inextricably linked with that of Bissier, for it was he who brought Bissier to world prominence through his pioneer exhibition at the Kestner-Gesellschaft, Hannover, and, of course, at the VI Bienal de São Paulo, Brazil, 1961.

The Federal Republic of Germany has been particularly interested and helpful in this project. Early in our preparations, Dr. Erich Franz Sommer, Cultural Affairs Officer for the San Francisco Consulate, arranged for my visit to Germany. Subsequently, Dr. Haide Russell, Consul for Cultural Affairs, of the Consulate in New York, collaborated to assist the publication of this catalogue. Mr. and Mrs. John Lefebre have also been most helpful in the various stages of preparation. The participation of Mrs. Duncan Phillips, Director, The Phillips Collection, Washington D.C.; Mr. Leon A. Arkus, Director, Museum of Art, Carnegie Institute, Pittsburgh; and Mr. Merrill C. Rueppel, Director, Dallas Museum of Fine Arts, is gratefully acknowledged. Suzanne Foley, Curator of the San Francisco Museum of Art, has been of invaluable assistance in the arrangement of loans, the preparation of the chronology, bibliography and related materials, and, with Beth Alberty of The Solomon R. Guggenheim Museum, has supervised the catalogue through final drafts to publication. We are also grateful to E. B. Ashton for his translations of the excerpts from Bissier's Journal.

Finally, on behalf of all of us who have been involved in the exhibition and the catalogue, a special salute to Mr. Thomas M. Messer, Director of The Solomon R. Guggenheim Museum, for his wholehearted participation in the development of the exhibition and for his personal contribution—the biographical essay and critical appraisal which he has written for this publication.

Gerald Nordland, Director
San Francisco Museum of Art

CHRONOLOGY

1839	Born December 3 in Freiburg-im-Breisgau, Germany.
1913	Studies art history at University of Freiburg-im-Breisgau.
1914	Attends Academy of Art in Karlsruhe for several months.
1914-18	Military service.
from 1918	Independent development as a painter.
1919	Introduction to Far Eastern art through friendship with Ernst Grosse, Orientalist at the University of Freiburg.
1920	First one-man exhibition at Kunstverein, Freiburg-im-Breisgau.
1928	Purchase of several works by Prussian government. Awarded Gold Medal in "Deutsche Kunst," Düsseldorf, and First Prize in Deutsche Künstlerbund, Kunstverein, Hannover.
1929-33	Teaches at University of Freiburg-im-Breisgau.
1929	Beginning of long friendship with Willi Baumeister.
1930	Visits Paris; meets Brancusi. Begins making India ink brush drawings, which he continues almost exclusively until 1947.
1933	Beginning of close friendship with Oskar Schlemmer.
1934	Destruction by fire of nearly all his work at University of Freiburg-im-Breisgau. Political situation not conducive to exhibitions of his work until 1947.
1935-38	Visits to Italy.
1939	Moves from Freiburg-im-Breisgau to Hagnau on Lake Constance.
from 1939	Designs for tapestries and fabrics which are woven by his wife, Lisbeth. Begins making woodcuts.
1947	First color monotypes.
1953	Transition to painting in egg-oil tempera (works since destroyed by artist).
1956	Paints "miniatures" in watercolor and egg-oil tempera on canvas.
from 1957	Annual visits to southern Switzerland.
1958	First major museum retrospective exhibition at the Kestner-Gesellschaft, Hannover, which travels to four other German museums, establishing his reputation internationally.

1959	Awarded Cornelius Prize of the City of Düsseldorf. Beginning of friendship with Hans Arp and Ben Nicholson in Switzerland.
1959-60	Designs outdoor mural for University of Freiburg-im-Breisgau.
1960	Awarded the "São Paulo Museum Prize" at the XXX Biennale, Venice, and Art Prize, Berlin.
1961	Awarded "Jubilee Prize" at the VI Bienal de São Paulo. Member of the Berlin Academy of Arts. Honorary member of the Nuremberg Academy of Arts.
late 1961	Moves to Ascona, Switzerland. Begins friendship with Mark Tobey.
1962	Receives Belgian Art Critics Prize.
1963	Named Professor by the government of Baden-Württemberg.
1964	Awarded Art Prize, Nordrhein-Westfalen.
1965	Dies June 18 in Ascona, Switzerland.

Julius Bissier in 1959

98. 11 August 60 drei Kreuze. 1960. Contemporary Collection of The Cleveland Museum of Art.

Julius Bissier

By Thomas M. Messer, Director
The Solomon R. Guggenheim Museum

Color to match the sense of my works must be festive, grandly original, without esthetisizing adornments. In other words: large reds, whites, blacks, greens, browns, etc. See the hues of multicolored stones, of green leaves, of the wilting autumn foliage, the great light of sunrise and sunset, the steel-blue to purple of the sun's play on the lake . . . .

He who bears witness to life must have the courage to speak the language of life, to show the images of life unvarnished, and first of all and above all: to create with the intensity of life.[1]

85. 18.Febr.59.M.1959. Collection Erhart and Anita Kästner, Wolfenbüttel.

So wrote the fifty-four year old Julius Bissier at the end of 1947 when his work as a colorist had not yet seriously begun. The passage foretells the ultimate phase in Bissier's life, that of the watercolors and of the oil-temperas which, since its beginning in the mid-fifties, has gained increasing currency and brings to mind, more readily than any other, Bissier's name. Through instantly evident attributes—compelling poetic quality, great refinement of taste, superb technique—Bissier's late, masterful work exerted an immediate appeal when it was first presented in this country in 1961. After a lifelong history of almost unmitigated rejection, an unbelieving artist, a few years before his death, saw his work become coveted and a highly-prized collector's item. At the same time, this sudden success led to shallow evaluations, to premature and rather cursory stylistic identifications that failed to reflect the underlying broader origins of this late flowering. As the exhibition described by this catalogue should make apparent, Bissier's attainments of his last decade, his now-famous *miniatures* and his larger work in color, assumes its full visual significance only in relation to the entire oeuvre.

1 To begin with the end, there is Bissier's color: An almost blueless grey may extend subtly into magentas and violets. Dialogues between rose and beige may include, ever so distantly, a white muslin ground, itself not free from almost imperceptible tints. Then again, strong accents in green, red, or black, may counter tender tones to evoke through such contrast a mercurial fluidity of attitude and mood. Gold, Bissier's neutral, stabilizing hue, is applied often in mosaic fashion to add exquisite notes of preciousness. The tinted textures range from smooth, liquid, and porous to hard, opaque, and metallic, yielding surfaces that have the capacity to merge meaningfully with the play of color. The unity of content and form, the identity of means and meaning, is rarely as self-evident as in Bissier's work. An almost episodic significance in his intimate statements is determined by colors and textures, through interplay of painting and support, and through the subtle workings of his knowing brush. One would misread his work, therefore, were one to approach it merely as non-objective abstraction, since allusion to objects and to situations—an allusion that is subject to recognition and remembrance—is part and parcel of his creative thought and of his imagery. Among objects, containers in every variation, fruit and plant forms, transformed celestial bodies, and references to man and beast recur with regularity. The container, as bottle, jar, vase, bowl, lamp, or shell, is whole or fragmented, standing alone or in groups, separately defined or placed in contrast with others to bring to the fore its particular attributes. Inside and outside are sometimes clearly indicated, sometimes left in an ambiguous relationship to each other. The container contains and is in turn contained. Voids and cavities may enclose substances but these may again become wholly or in part enveloping outlines so that an unending game of dichotomies and dialectical resolutions ensues. The complementaries in such instances are objectified most often as bottles and fruit. The former may be more or less protective according to the opaqueness or the transparency of its walls, the visibility or invisibility of the shielded content, the wholeness or partiality of its contours, the smoothness or jaggedness of its outlines. Bissier's multi-directional picture space may be oriented concentrically or excentrically. The relationship from container to fruit implies a direction from without to within but an opposite sense of movement from within to without may also be in evi-

74. 23.X.56. Ascona MN. 1956. Collection Lisbeth Bissier, Ascona.

dence. Clover or plant forms, for example, press upon their seed-substance as star-shaped images float in a space in which expansions are determined by energies at the center. Then, tensions may suddenly be suspended as moons and suns hover gently around the bottles, linger weightlessly upon their narrow necks, turn imperceptibly into fruit and house forms and are eventually contained by the stillness of the surface.

75. 9.I.57. 1957. Collection Lisbeth Bissier, Ascona.

100. 19.Sept.60. K. 1960. Lent by Estate of the Artist.

118. 10.11.62 B Gamma. 1962. Lent by Estate of the Artist.

93. 14.September 59 Mona. 1959. Collection Lisbeth Bissier, Ascona.

Situations and moods too, run the gamut of our awareness. A gentle lyricism is prevalent, but ominous and aggressive images also may stretch out menacingly toward each other, toward fragile glass vases and the quietly maturing content within. There are sticks and crosses, flags and daggers that jointly inhabit a space that knows no up or down, no right or left, as if it had been created solely for Bissier's floating thoughts, his colored visions and for his symbolically predicated meditations. Inseparable from such materializations is the artist's signatory emblem, a circular cork imprint, adding a disc to the often circular imagery—a disc among discs, therefore, which seems to be saying: I, Bissier, who am a touch of blue on pink ground have merged by the will of an ever-moving power with other residues—shapes that are not much or a great deal, depending upon what you make of it. Finally, there is man, subsumed in other objects, in other thoughts and forms, but nevertheless recognizable, remembered, perhaps, by such nearly symmetrical images as would suggest, interchangeably, mouth, breasts, or buttocks, or through the willful movement of an advancing trunk shape which, by the slightest twist of a fluid imagination, may be turned into the bottle forms that remain ever ready to reassert themselves.

135. Dunkler Pfingsttag 61. 1961. Collection Mr. and Mrs. L. F. Gittler, New York.

Bissier himself was not unaware of the connections between the seen, observed and experienced on the one hand and the non-mimetic pictorial result on the other, as the following entry in his Journal shows:

Some forms in nature or in its states of transition are torn, others spongy, still others powdery. Some affect you agreeably, some disagreeably, as you observe them. Take such varied contrasts and project them onto a flat surface, whether in a "composition" or as handwritten notes accidentally jotted down. Think of such jottings as charged—well, with the way I am, and you have the essence of my works.

Now, if you imagine that even ideas can be combined with such notes—perhaps by arranging the surface characters in a particular set of conceptions such as vegetable, mineral, fire, earth, water, and their juxtaposition and opposition and mixture—you open up a second possibility. And if you go on to think that certain states of mind will make one prefer one "surface character" or the other, and that in such a state one will directly use the characters as compositions corresponding to one's "mood," you have what in my work I call a "metaphor."[2]

Content, in the sense recounted here, will at times come to terms with the absolute symbols of geometry. Circles, triangles, crescents, U-shapes, and others, detached now from their naturalistic connotations, thus become readable in a parallel context. From an examination of Bissier's work it is clear, however, that geometry was not usually the point of departure for his images and that as a discipline it failed him when he depended upon it for creative impulse. Not only are his forms too richly irregular and too freely deviating from the pure completeness of geometric concepts but his predilection for the organically *biotic* presents itself as an antithesis to geometric reduction. Aware of the alternative and of his own stance Bissier wrote:

Spontaneity, magic origins, Bios—here are the objectives of my work.[3]

or,

My works are a matter of spontaneously, not calculatedly, invented form—that is the gist of it. And therein I am closer to expressionism than to the purism of a Mondrian, a Bill, etc.[4]

and again,

Whenever I leave the biocentric, all but microscopic form in favor of an abstract formalism I get Paul Klees, Baumeisters, little Légers. The micro-macrocosmic image, or possibly the biotic symbol—that's for me.[5]

26. 4.10.48 Viereck und Dreieck. 1948.
Collection Lisbeth Bissier, Ascona.

Lastly, letters and ideograms, not infrequently as reversed mirror images, add themselves to objects, to signs and symbols, and to geometric forms without a sense of intrusion and entirely on equal terms. The Greek alphabet with its Alphas and Omegas, its Epsilons and Taus, singly or in combination so as to insinuate but never furnish literal meanings, is a conspicuous source for the lettered presences. These form a part of the same picture-script, of that same no man's land between painting and writing that covers the surface at large, which then receives a final validation through the ample signature and the unselfconsciously scribbled date—both applied as if the work were formally incomplete without such broadly brushed additions.

99. 14 August 60 K. 1960. Collection Marion Lefebre, New York.

2 The ease and detachment in Bissier's late work is deceiving. There are probably few modern painters to whom color came so hard and who at the same time needed it as desperately for their ultimate fulfillment as he did. Even to Paul Klee, who constitutes an irremovable and in some ways oppressive presence in the life of his younger contemporary, color revealed itself only after tenacious youthful struggles, suddenly and as if by miracle, upon his return from a Tunisian journey in 1914, when the 35-year old artist recorded the following much-quoted entry in his diary: "Color possesses me, I don't have to pursue it. It will possess me always, I know it. That is the meaning of this happy hour: Color and I are one, I am a painter."[6] By contrast, in Bissier's mature phase, tentative yearnings to extend an already highly developed quasi-oriental ink drawing into a coloristic dimension are not recorded until 1943 at the age of 50. His Journal, which in its continuous form began only a year before the earliest entry quoted here, reflects an ever-present urge for coloristic fulfillment as well as a sense of inadequacy and a puritanical inhibition toward color as the "seductress," the undermining agent that could lead him astray from the "sacred" content of his black and white art toward mere "peinture"—in his view an engaging but shallow surface manifestation that might assure a much-desired success at the price of inner corruption. Entries in Bissier's Journal return to this tension between an instinctual need for color and a chaste fear with obsessive regularity, as the following quotations selected from a great many that bear upon the same subject will show:

9.11.43 *I believe that now, after several years, I have at last abandoned the Japanese formula of my works. A simple technical change from India ink to the use of a color paste made up of English red, glazing + sand, used frequently if not yet consciously (in the years of 29-33), brought the new form which corresponds more closely to the biotic tenor of my purposes than does the all too Eastern medium of the inks.*

11.11.43 *An error—I have gone back to India ink. I can't do without civilization, despite will and reasoning.*

24/25.5.44 *Succeeded with the first translations from India ink into color, and at last found the technical formula: oil used in water color fashion, with a lot of turpentine on rubbed colored canvas. It works exactly like the inks—and how long I have been searching for a way to free the inks from their Japanoid entanglement.*

1.6.44 *In the last few days one small canvas daily. Today a coloristically most charming one. It will take much experimentation to get some of the unshakable finality of the inks into these color transcriptions.*

23.12.45 *Working like mad from morning to night. Good sheets in pastel and chalk. Pleasant splashing in colors and lines, on themes like those of the inks. The feeling a bit sinful, more shallow: an escape from the holy earnest of the inks... Whether the moral value is the same I cannot tell now...The "inks" unquestionably have something sacred about them—the new works are late peinture, that much is clear. But a little ease feels good for the moment.*
Late at night: *The monk will renounce that little transgression into the flowering fields of life. He will return to God!*

6.10.46 *...Surprising new technique—the inks in color, totally, completely adequate. Transfer oils liquidly painted on glass. If this should not last either, the dream of colored inks is at an end.*

8.10.46...*After a few days, and renewed efforts to make colored inks, back to the old black India ink. Color simply robs them of the desired sacred touch.*

31.10.46 *Three colored abstractions, including one that promises further possibilities if by tomorrow it does not disappoint again....But why do I keep feeling drawn there: is it because color would bring an expansion of the symbols, the metaphors—in short, an organ instead of a shepherd's flute...?*

17.2.47...*discovery that it is possible to achieve the sacred character with a few spots of color solely by the vibrant monochromatic ground...A big discovery that must become second nature.*
Late at night: Found *the definitive* translation of *inks into pastel or chalk color. Oil print.*

18.2.47 Lost *the definitive. For me there is no final finding in this life.*

19.2.47 *Found it after all—full-value translation. Prints, oil on paper.*

31.8.47 *A series of visitors—whose judgment I'd have to respect if I weren't my own jack of the trade—pronounced the inks "unique." But now I find that the world they came out of, the inner world of their birth, so to speak, is extinct. I feel driven toward greater gaiety, more abundant composition, greater balance.*

25.12.47 *Two days of obsessive work have today brought the* definitive large color format *of the inks. The miniatures were the precursors. Now that the first large sheets are here I knock on my forehead and ask myself how this simplest of things could possibly take me 4 years. The asset column of my artist's life will finally add up: in the 6th decade a result which others are given in their 3rd! Be that as it may, I am grateful, and I see the inevitability of my development in all the phases of my many-stationed life. The inks, however...but the inks here... here the game ends, and "the gray of infinity" (winter) has mastered color, property of "the generations of earth" (winter).*

Throughout, the Journal is ahead of its time and refers to attainments that were fully consummated only in subsequent years. Regrettably, it ends before Bissier's color comes into its own, having finally overcome the partly self-generated obstacles that had hampered its emergence. If there is nothing quite as unequivocal in Bissier's statements as Klee's "Color and I are one. I am a painter," there is nevertheless the late Journal entry of February 2, 1948 made, again, about works which in hindsight must be relegated to inconclusive and tentative essays:

25.2.48 *Once more working in a state of grace. One sheet more radiant, more festive, more flowery than the next. Such days find me full of heartfelt thanks to fate. These new works* must *be successful: they haven't a trace of the gloom of the inks that menaces the Germans.*

However, doubts about the ultimate validity of the color works as opposed to the inks never wholly left Bissier. Its general acceptance notwithstanding, Bissier, on the occasion of his New York shows at the Lefebre Gallery in the 1960's, expressed full confidence in the durability of his *tusches* (the term by which the artist referred to his brushwork in black India ink) while asking anxious questions about the validity of his late work in color. The struggle to break away from the "Chinese" limitations of the India ink medium into a broader and more telling color mode was perhaps never entirely overcome, even if we may feel today that the end result is an unqualified triumph signifying the fulfillment of Bissier's creative potential.

3 The transformation of Bissier's work from black and white to color led through complex technical stages to which the artist ascribed considerable importance. Besides such conventional approaches as pastels or colored chalk, Bissier mentions: oil used in the manner of turpentine on rubbed canvas; liquid transfers printed in oils upon glass; color pastes made up of English red, glazing and sand; incisions in burned bricks; casein-sand inks; and modifications from print to direct pen drawing with watercolor upon printed grounds. Prints, approached tentatively in the mid-forties and developed consistently in 1947, fulfilled a role in the transition toward color that can hardly be exaggerated as the following diary excerpts, again selected from among a great many more on the same subject, indicate:

29.11.46 At the moment, amid horrid spasms of my external and internal life, occasional work on "glass prints." A possibility whose definitive evaluation is not yet clear to me....

25.2.47 Each print more beautiful than the next. Could the synthesis have come at last in secrecy and silence, like health? This has nothing to do any more with the experiments in oil and pastel, with any kind of "peinture." Here a note which may be subtler than that of the inks has matured in spirit, and again in the spirit of the East.

19.8.47 First attempts with linoleum cuts in the manner of the (small) colored miniatures of this year. The same questions and doubts as when I started the miniatures.

41. 48 (18). 1948. Lent by Estate of the Artist.

49. 49 II/6. Lent by Estate of the Artist.

13.9.47 *Experimenting wildly with direct prints instead of the woodcuts of the past 3 weeks. Where is the daemonic order of the inks? The Satan of reproduction is having a field day....*

12.1.48 *The year began with rich work.* The "translation" of the inks into large-scale colored monotypes has been perfected technically and spiritually. *The dubious side of the miniatures is overcome. Now the door to color stands wide open: the plus of color can be added to the symbols in ink. Another milestone in my life has been reached. One of the final stones....*

17.1.48 *The technique of the prints is absolutely under control, so there is no question any more: the means have at last been achieved.*
I feel I have found my final, definitive mode of expression parallel to the inks. Now the work can be completed, expanded, ripened, magnified—for the addition of color is a gain beyond doubt, and without losing the timelessness of the inks. The print was the entire secret. "Painting" won't do it; it would become peinture.

Despite the undeniable importance for the gradual conquest of color, prints seem an uncongenial medium in Bissier's hands when compared with the sure brushwork in black and white or in color. In the first place, the production of replicas created a new "ethical" problem for the anti-commercial (and therefore anti-multiple) artist who, concentrating upon monotype, made sure that no one impression would be identical with another—thereby contriving to subvert the basic print idea. But in addition, the painstaking and indirect technique which Bissier developed from his work on glass was so totally opposed to the compressed summarizations of the inks, that entirely new working and thinking habits had to be cultivated over an extended period of time before the result would correspond to the objective. Such labors eventually bore fruit in the colored work of Bissier's last decade, when water-colors, oil temperas in miniature and in bigger formats came in large numbers. These same exertions failed, however, to impart to the much earlier prints the sense of control and detachment that Bissier sought.

The emergence and the eventual conquest of color which came via print experiments as a slow and painful secession from India inks did not displace the brushwork in black and white. Rather did the latter serve as a safe base from which sorties into the always treacherous color terrain were undertaken—a base that also could be used as a retreat whenever the lines of communication toward

new experimentation became too tenuous. Although in the last decade of his life the productive balance swung from the inks to the various color media, Bissier abandoned the forced ejection of psychograms only at the very end when he began to feel that the intensive mental concentration needed to compress pictorial ideas within a single stroke exceeded his strength. It is therefore quite deliberate and in keeping with Bissier's own value judgements that this exhibition places heavy emphasis upon the so-called *tusches* since these constitute the nourishing soil for Bissier's late flowering.

23. 1940 Blütenentfaltung III. 1940. Lent by Estate of the Artist.

4 Like the work already discussed, the black brushwork in India ink is also more varied than cursory acquaintance may suggest. There is, first of all, a distinct difference between those completed between the mid-thirties and the mid-forties on the one hand, and those that began around 1947, to run concurrently with Bissier's colored work. In general, the earlier examples may be described as "symbolic," the later as "tachist" or "expressionist." Imagery in the earlier work relies on a number of basic themes which then are subject to variations and to reinterpretations. Among them symbols of the male and female dualism and of its ultimate unity are most pervasive. Aggression and defense, protrusion, envelopment, unification and separation—movement, in other words, that rises beyond the restricted sexual application onto the grand rhythms of all living—find particular utilization as form-content in works entitled for example, "seed pod," "fruit stand," "two forms," "threatened seeds," "guarded fruit," "penetration," "touching and warding-off," etc. Through these and other comparable designations Bissier makes

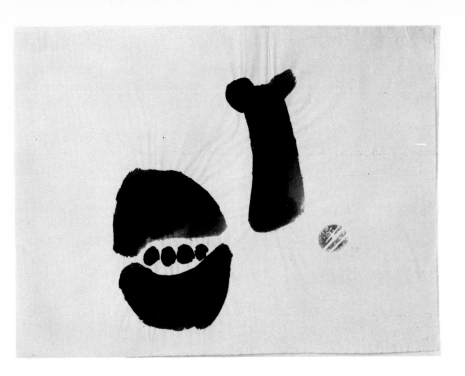

28. Muschel 49. 1949. Lent by Estate of the Artist.
29. 19.4.58. 1958. Collection Lisbeth Bissier, Ascona.

explicit his graphic preoccupation with the life-giving organic processes or, as he calls them repeatedly, the *biotic* foundations of his private universe. Further reduced to components, the symbols, partly drawn from the writings of the German philosopher Johann-Jakob Bachofen (brought to Bissier's attention in 1938) refer to swamps, to the double aspects in nature epitomized by the twin sign, to the egg with its complementary halves, the egg as embryonic life, the circle as a channel of recurrent flow, the cross as a meeting of horizontals and verticals that recalls a parallel polarity of man and woman, and many other graphic concepts with more or less self-evident symbolic application. So involved with

philosophical contemplation is Bissier at the time that an early entry in the Journal places his work beyond painting as ordinarily conceived:

The work with the inks develops more and more in a poetic, metaphysical direction. As painting in the usual sense of the word it is no longer comprehensible, not even with abstract painting having gone academic in the meantime.[7]

It is difficult not to stress philosophy as a nourishing substance in Bissier's work. It is all the more important, however, to re-establish a proper balance by drawing attention to Bissier's complementary realization that understands painting as ultimately manual and instinctual and comprehends particular insights as something that must be filtered through an acquired control over materials and techniques. Left as "sedimentation," then, is a spiritual state, transformed into material residues that contain the essence of Bissier's creative personality. Analysts of Bissier's art have rightly stressed the directness and the autonomy of his painterly impulses and rejected any implication of "translation" from verbal into

5. männl./weibl. Einheitszeichen 38.3. 1938. Lent by Estate of the Artist.

pictorial concepts. Dr. Werner Schmalenbach, who brought Bissier's late work to worldwide attention through a series of memorable exhibitions in Germany and abroad, writes the following pertinent passage in the monograph devoted to the artist:

Were one to risk a misconception fatal for any artist, one would say that Bissier's art is philosophical. Not that he philosophized as a painter: he speaks the pure language of painting and no other. But much as he is concerned with pictures, each of his pictures is meaningful; where meaning is not revealed, the image for him—and for us— is not fully valid.[8]

By the same token, references to Bissier's "symbols" make it imperative to restate the distinction between an overt, and therefore interpretable, symbolism (which had no place in Bissier's work from the early 1930's on) and a reliance upon a subjectively developed picture script with symbolic connotations which Bissier developed for himself in an almost Oriental manner. *Symbolism,* as Kurt Leonhart points out in an early critical evaluation of Bissier's work, "is as distinct from a symbolically predicated art as realism is from reality, or existentialism from existence."[9]

By comparison with the late works of the forties and with subsequent work, the symbolic inks that fall roughly between 1936 and 1946 are clearly defined and relatively static whereas their successors are seemingly formless and explosively dynamic. Depending, in characteristic instances, on a double image in a state of interdependence, the symbolic inks bear almost without exception the small round cork imprint which never fails to draw the viewer into the orbit of Bissier's presence without betraying its purely visual function as an integral part of the paper surface. In the works beginning with the late

17. Granatäpfel 42. 1942. Lent by Estate of the Artist.

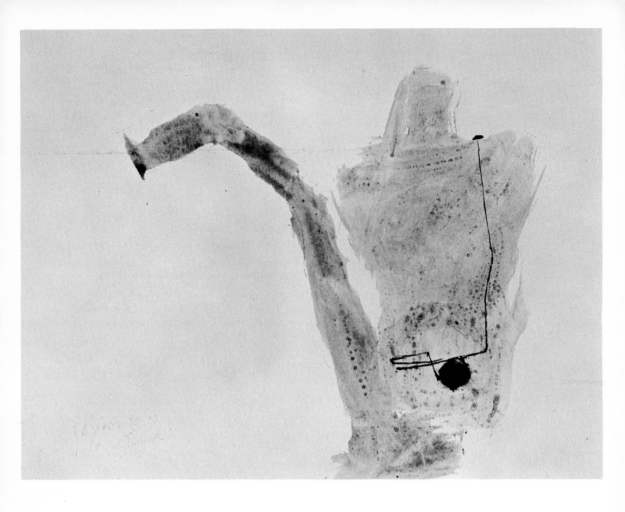

30. 26.febr.59 y. 1959. Lent by Estate of the Artist.

1940's, however, all symbolic content recedes as meanings merge with the act of painting. With an increase of speed and an ever-growing release of concentrated tension, Bissier reached for home-made brushes that through the addition of "joints" would follow the slightest turn of his guiding hand. Titles become rarer and eventually disappear altogether so that the always prominent date, the frequent indication of locale, and an occasional dedication become the sole identifying feature. The central concepts in Bissier's inks are "biotic," a term referring to the vital, organic, life-nourishing forces, and "theistic," which connotes a broadly-based spiritual orientation toward a Supreme Being. "Biotic-theistic" *in conjunction* would seem to express the ultimate identity of the organic world with the transcendental kinetic order which Bissier places under his "God of all movement." Commenting about the brush drawings in his Journal, Bissier reaffirmed again and again their pivotal position in his whole oeuvre—a conviction which he did not abandon even when the subsequent color work signalled the breakthrough which he had so passionately desired.

24/25.6.44 All recent colored experiments suddenly seem like games again, relatively speaking. A comparison I made with the inks of the past years shows that the inks are my singular and inescapable fate as an artist.

20.8.46 Today ink upon ink. 3 large-sized ones after some 20 sheets on the same subject. The sheet "Egg and Cloud" came out strikingly. The awful materialism of the past few days drives me back to my cell.

36. 18.II.61 Wu. 1961. Lent by Estate of the Artist.

The inks and the colored work represent polarities—indeed a dichotomy in Bissier's oeuvre of which he was fully aware. The contrast between the two is apprehensible on three levels: in the visual difference, in the working attitude, and as a philosophical contradiction. Leaving aside visual differences as self-evident and the philosophical contradictions as speculative, it may be well to stress again how each type came about. The paintings, having their technical origins in monotypes, were created through a process in which meditated motions would place stroke upon stroke in a self-forgetful, detached and unhurried process guided by Bissier's increasingly sure intuition. While there are better and lesser works, the standard of accomplishment was even and in good working spells the artist could turn out one sheet a day with the sense of effortless inevitability that made him turn his eyes upward upon completion to ad-

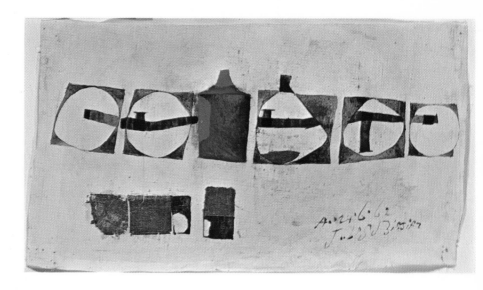

116. A 24.6.62. 1962. Collection Mrs. Robert M. Benjamin, New York.

73. 14.III.56. 1956. Lent by Estate of the Artist.
57. deo gratias Ronco 18.X.59 N. 1959. Lent by Estate of the Artist.

35. 4.4.60.XI. 1960. Lent by Galerie Beyeler, Basel.
39. H 4.März 64. 1964. Lent by Estate of the Artist.

dress a "Danke" to the power of whose will he considered himself to be an instrument. The ink drawings, by contrast, and particularly those created concurrently with the watercolors and oil-temperas, were neither slowly gathered, nor in that sense detached, but the result of an intense state of inner tension involving every fiber of the artist's being. From the beginning, the qualitative standard in this medium ranges from fully accomplished, inspired examples, to total failures, and Bissier, aware of such a broad range, exercised a relentless censorship upon his own output. His widow reports that in his earlier work Bissier would habitually complete 50 to 100 inks in quick sequence all oriented toward one theme and keep, upon reflection, not more than two to three per cent—a ratio of destruction which, to be sure, decreased markedly in his later work. In view of the strains and the excessive concentration required in such a working process the gradual turn toward the meditative surfaces in watercolor and oil-tempera may perhaps also have constituted a compensating alternative for the time when the strength to function in flashlike bursts would have spent itself. Whether this was so intended or not, is of course difficult to establish, but as a matter of fact it did happen that way with Julius Bissier.

15. aufprallende Woge I 1939. 1939. Lent by Estate of the Artist.

5 Bissier's free and accomplished painting in India ink did not, of course, stand at the beginning of his development but was itself the result of a persistent striving, analogous in many ways to that exerted later in the attempt to comprehend and apply color. Not too promising in his initial essays, the 20-year old Bissier produced some realistic portraiture that was followed by vaguely expressionist figure and landscape painting. From the scant existing remnants one may gather how difficult the beginnings were and how bewildering Bissier must have found the early impact of current and historic styles. The very first inks, now traced back to 1926, were executed in Bissier's home-made solutions that gave him a wide tonal range from deep black to light grey with much nuance in between. It was not before the early 1930's, however, that surrealist and cubist elements with echoes from the Italian *Pittura Metaphysica* and the German *Neue Sachlichkeit* led him toward a vocabulary which, like that of the styles he reflected, depended upon the poignancy of the object placed in an illusionistic space. Although concept and execution at that time began to gain in self-assurance, Bissier's work still leaned upon the Constructivists, the Dadaists, Moore, Léger, and his compatriot Willi Baumeister while only isolated examples foretold the uniqueness of his later phases.

Unlike the "Chinese" brushwork that eventually evolved, the initial inks were nature-bound, surrealistic in their use of illusionist depth and overtly symbolic in content. Symbolism, while not readily convertible into literary meanings, nevertheless referred to the anguished prewar era with its psychic tensions and its manifestations of fear.

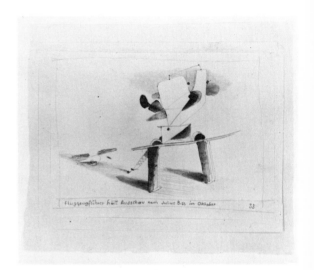

ill. a. zwei früheste Zeugnisse. *(Not in exhibition)*

ill. b. flugzeugführer hält Ausschau nach Julius Biss im Oktober 33. 1933. *(Not in exhibition)*

Thus, the years from 1931, when "symbols" in a more restricted sense were first rendered in India ink, to 1936, when these began to assume their biotic character, are crucial and the break that took place then seems even more accentuated with hindsight. Between those dates, in 1934, occur two tragic events: the death of Bissier's son and the destruction of his work in a fire at the Freiburg University that consumed his studio. These events must be seen against the political background of Hitler's rise which reached an early climax in the dictator's full assumption of political powers in 1933.

Concurrently with the now-abstract ink painting which Bissier began behind drawn blinds to avoid official interest in what Nazi Germany called "degenerate" art, he completed a sequence which he himself termed "surreal" in which he subsumed fateful experiences of a personal as well as of a general kind. The death of his child, the Spanish Civil War, and the then-current situation in Germany mirrored themselves in these works. Like Klee, Moore, or Picasso, though less freely and convincingly than those grand masters who in the 1930's were the prophetic generation, Bissier renders proof of a clairvoyance—of a fundamental awareness of the issues of his time and of a capacity to find formal analogies for them. By 1935-36, however, this intermediary phase gave way to the new idiom as Bissier's forms flattened, and as his partly inherited symbolism was replaced by a psychogramatic expression of extraordinary power and originality. Bissier was aware of the break that occurred in these years and quite understandably located its critical moment in 1934—the year of calamity. "I found myself as an artist at the deathbed of my son," he said according to his widow. In the years that followed, Bissier's imagery was fully developed through a prodigious output that obliterated the distinctions between painting and writing. Progressing toward a reduction of the symbolic component, Bissier's art moved gradually in the direction of tachist abstraction which toward the late 1940's assumed legible form in the parallel striving of contemporary artists on both sides of the Atlantic.

ill. c. Korallen II. *(Not in exhibition)*

ill. d. Gefässe I. *(Not in exhibition)*

6 In speaking of Bissier in this Introduction, I have proceeded backwards, as it were, beginning with his best known and latest work in which, after a decade of struggle, color came into its own. This late emergence may be seen against the background of brush drawings in India ink which throughout his mature development were the mainstay of Bissier's art. An overt symbolism that placed its objects within a surreal space, a mode still indebted to the pace-setting invention between the wars, was then considered as a preamble to Bissier's original contributions. Hidden behind such developments, far withdrawn from the autonomous existence of the work itself, is Bissier the man, about whom some comments may now be in order.

Relatively few people whose testimony is valuable to us today knew the extremely retiring artist through personal contact. Because of this, Bissier's unpublished and largely untranslated Journal assumes particular importance even though its irregular entries, apart from isolated fragments, are limited to the years between 1942 and 1949. During these dificult times, the artist and his small family circle were leading an isolated and fearful existence, threatened as they were by the internal tyranny of the Nazi regime, by Allied bombing raids, the advancing armies of liberation, and eventually, by a French military government. The Journal, is therefore, in part at least, a moving account of human fate, caught and engulfed by the impersonal destructiveness of a larger conflict—an account often raised from personal to general validity through Bissier's articulate and philosophically disciplined mind. Throughout the Journal pages, acute insights are derived from preoccupations with his own and his family's safety, from concerns for the weal of the world, and from his art which is nothing to Bissier if not visual analogy or form-parable to human situations.

The range of general subjects touched upon in this spontaneously kept diary, besides the running account of personal and creative developments, is very wide. War and peace, the fate of Germany, the position of the artist, art and commerce, as well as poetry, music, philosophy and theology are among recurrent themes. Besides his struggles for technical and formal solutions and the related self-evaluations as man and artist, the Journal returns most often to religious questions, to relationships with other artists and their work, and to problems posed by Oriental art and thought. The subjects, of course, are frequently interrelated and inseparably interwoven.

Two conspicuous misconceptions about his work gave

Bissier cause not only for frequent rebuttals but also for some anguish and bitterness. One was the often stated assumption that he was in essence a Chinese calligrapher, the other, equally injurious, was the false link established between his work and that of Paul Klee.

The differences between Klee and Bissier are so numerous and of such a fundamental nature that an attempt to render them here would lead too far. Let it therefore be said merely that Klee's wider range depended upon the successful integration of expressive and constructive components, upon a painterly intuition steeped in a complex grammar of form, and upon the effective elimination of dividing lines between figuration and non-objective abstraction. By comparison Bissier's scope is more restricted and his works, despite a high degree of variation, are the outcome of a single-minded quest, first for the formulation of symbols, and ultimately, for a painterly script which, through an exceptional degree of detached control, evokes a softly spoken world-view of considerable consequence. Although there are obvious kinships and certain parallels in attitudes and motivation, there is no Bissier that looks remotely like a Klee and Bissier's irritation with an irrelevant juxtaposition is therefore well-founded. Among numerous passages in the Journal, one that expresses an aspect of the stated differences with precision, although not without an undertone of bitterness, states:

There is no comparing Paul Klee's work and my symbols. For Klee deals in travesties (grotesque disguises...) while my works aim to be true "signs."[10]

Even more complicated is Bissier's relationship to Oriental art. As early as 1927 he was introduced to the art of East Asia through his friendship with the Orientalist Ernst

148. a.6.Juni 64. 1964. Lent by Estate of the Artist.

Grosse, who helped to bring to the surface an evidently latent response to Oriental stimuli. Critics, fellow artists and friends were all too ready to pounce upon the obvious, thereby forcing Bissier into an oral and written defense posture:

...Why shouldn't I grow skeptical about being understood despite my own unshakable faith in the inks?...They all take the inks for "Chinese"! As if there were a spark of China in that, apart from the ink-painting technique. In any case, there is nothing in it of which the Chinese himself would say: It's Chinese. If I paint the same inks in color, nobody will call them Chinese any more....

And he continues in his typically self-accusatory fashion:

. . . You, sir, are unfortunately not Chinese, or all this would not excite you; it could not touch you at all. It is only ambition that lurks in you still (and how!)—otherwise you would withdraw to the company of Bachofen and Meyer-Amden and Hölderlin, fully aware that the present ones can't understand you because you came closer to the core of things than they ....[11]

Bissier's argument is well taken even if it stands to reason that his great interest in Oriental thought and religion enlarged his creative personality and returned to his essentially Western art elements acquired through familiarity with the East. There are other passages in the Journal that treat the "Chinese question" more positively.

Reading Bachofen's theory of immortality. Amazed to see the whole theory of a Beyond and the moralism of Christianity spread from a blend of Neo-Platonism with the age-old Near Eastern myths. At the same time, recognizing that I stand on entirely different soil, I finally get an intellectual grasp on my stronger leaning to the East, i.e., to the Y Ging as the theory of total cosmic change without moral doctrines. The spirit as the emanating center of a metamorphosis incessantly projected into the material realm. The above and below of Neo-Platonism, the migration of individual speech from the terrestrial to "heaven" and back—not valid for me....[12]

The existing ambiguity in Bissier's relationship to Oriental art may also be seen in the following two contradictory passages in which he first shuns and then accepts the written painting of the East for his own purposes:

The inks are too civilized for my purpose, too reminiscent of Chinese calligraphy. With the new technique there is no such danger.[13]

And on the other hand:

...It is clear too that oil painting is not for me, though distantly part of my orbit. What intrigues me time and again is the script with its Eastern connotations.[14]

To conclude: There cannot be any doubt that superficial resemblances as well as deeply-rooted correspondences between some Chinese idioms and Bissier's inked brush work exist. The mindless confusion of one with the other, however, amounts to a misconception which the artist had every reason to resent.

7 *Since the beginning of the year I have been working like a man with life on his mind and death at his heels.... If only the dread of life, the legacy of a depressive father, did not constantly peer in the window like an evil specter...Who could help a tortured animal like me, and how could help come?*[15]

...Learn to wait, Mr. Seismograph! But the will to live?[16]

Passages like these, written some 18 years before Bissier's death give an inkling of the artist's morbid preoccupations. It is true that Bissier had his share of calamity in his lifetime and therefore, his pessimistic outlook is not altogether surprising. Suffering from diabetes and from heart, liver and kidney ailments, and pursued by a flock of trivial conditions, his hypochondriac disposition always led him to expect the worst. In this he was aided by a fecund imagination that found no difficulty in filling in the gory details. To his own amazement, however, he survived internal collapse and external destruction to live into his 72nd year. Working to the last day he was eventually felled by a small stroke. From the Journals and from other acounts Bissier emerges as a sensitive, anxious man who sees life pessimistically from an elevated ethical vista. Dedicated to his art and incapable of compromise he was doubtful of his capacities and according to his own admissions, overly concerned with the reactions of outsiders, whether qualified or not. Toward his art he was exceedingly severe, deprecatory and protective at the same time. A man of considerable mental clarity, Bissier was able to condense and articulate thought in a crystalline manner and his Journal abounds with precisely formulated issues and his responses to them.

In the end, Bissier characterizes himself best. With the same detachment that has brought forth the autonomy of the inks, the watercolors, and the oil-tempera works of his late maturity, he writes about himself as objectively as if he were someone else:

The eve of the anniversary of my father's death. Forty years have since passed, and heaven has kept me thus far. Was it my parents' blessing? I am convinced there is a great deal to this word. But with increasing age I feel my father's somber nature expand in me. His melancholia, his anxiety, his excessive worry for his life. No matter; I owe him a highminded idealism, a searching curiosity, a love of absolute truthfulness. Two days from now it will be 19 years that my mother died—she who gave me my other part: the gift of observation, the urge to analyze people, the inner unrest, the ambition, and the pride of the lonely who come to hate humanity because they love it. And the tenacity to cling to gains once made, whether to spiritual or to material possessions. What is problematical in me derives from her. And, of this I'm sure, from her father....[17]

Hand of the artist.

1 Julius Bissier's *Journal,* an unpublished manuscript in the possession of the artist's widow, Mrs. Lisbeth Bissier (Ascona, Switzerland), covers the years from 1942 through 1949. As the *Journal* is not paginated, the entries are listed under their corresponding dates, as here: *Journal,* 28.12.47

2 *Ibid.,* 18.1.47

3 *Ibid.,* 16.2.47

4 *Ibid.,* 2.2.47

5 *Ibid.,* 8.3.47

6 Klee, Paul, *The Diaries of Paul Klee, 1898-1918,* ed. Felix Klee, University of California, Berkeley, California, 1964, p. 297

7 *Journal,* 22.3.46

8 Schmalenbach, Werner, *Bissier,* Gerd Hetje, Stuttgart, 1963, p. 6

9 Leonhart, Kurt, *Julius Bissier,* Kunstverlag KG Dieter Keller & Cie, Stuttgart, 1948

10 *Journal,* 30.5.44

11 *Ibid.,* 16.11.47

12 *Ibid.,* 7.9.46

13 *Ibid.,* 9.11.43

14 *Ibid.,* 8.3.47

15 *Ibid.,* 1.8.47

16 *Ibid.,* 18.7.47

17 *Ibid.,* 2.3.47

WORKS IN THE EXHIBITION

For the sake of unambiguous identification, dates and inscriptions, taken as exactly as possible from the original works or from photographs of them, have been used as titles, and no attempt at translation has been made.

Dimensions are given in both inches and centimeters. Measurements were made in centimeters and converted to inches to the nearest eighth of an inch.

Height precedes width.

The works are listed in seven groups, by media and size.

Unless otherwise indicated, works are lent by the Estate of the Artist.

1. 37 Fruchtträger, archaisch Kypsele. 1937.
Lent by Estate of the Artist.

SMALL-FORMAT BRUSH DRAWINGS, INDIA INK ON JAPANESE PAPERS

1. 37 Fruchtträger, archaisch Kypsele. 1937.
   10 x 6¾" (25.2 x 17 cm.)
2. 37 'frucht'. 1937.
   9⅞ x 7¼" (25 x 18.3 cm.)
3. Töpferbild 37. 1937.
   6⅝ x 9¾" (16.9 x 24.7 cm.)
4. 37 männl./weibl. Einheitszeichen. 1937.
   9⅞ x 6⅝" (25 x 16.7 cm.)
5. männl./weibl. Einheitszeichen 38.3. 1938.
   6¾ x 9⅞" (17 x 25.1 cm.)
6. 38 archaisch:Ei. (werden und vergehen = weiss schwarz). 1938.
   9¾ x 6⅝" (24.6 x 16.9 cm.)
7. 38 Nest im Dornbusch. 1938.
   10 x 6¾" (25.2 x 17.2 cm.)
8. 38 Durchdringung. 1938.
   6⅞ x 9⅝" (17.3 x 24.5 cm.)
9. Antikes Symbol von Oknos dem Seilflechter 38. 1938.
   9⅞ x 7⅜" (25 x 18.6 cm.)
10. Gelenkartig 38. 1938.
    9¾ x 6⅝" (24.6 x 16.9 cm.)
11. 38 (20862). 1938.
    9⅜ x 6¼" (23.7 x 15.9 cm.)
12. Cista 39.2. 1939.
    9⅝ x 6⅝" (24.5 x 16.8 cm.)
13. 39 Samenkapsel. 1939.
    6¾ x 9¾" (17 x 24.8 cm.)
14. Töpferzeichnung 39. 1939.
    6¾ x 9¾" (17 x 24.6 cm.)
15. aufprallende Woge I 1939. 1939.
    6¾ x 9¾" (17.2 x 24.6 cm.)
16. Schwebend gegen fest 40. 1940.
    6¼ x 9⅜" (15.8 x 23.8 cm.)
17. Granatäpfel 42. 1942.
    6¼ x 9⅜" (15 x 23.8 cm.)
18. 43 gebend empfangend. 1943.
    9½ x 6¼" (24 x 15.9 cm.)
19. Schreckauge über Frucht 43. 1943.
    6¼ x 9½" (15.8 x 24 cm.)

LARGE-FORMAT BRUSH DRAWINGS, INDIA INK ON JAPANESE PAPERS

20. 38.I. 1938.
    24⅜ x 18⅞" (62 x 48 cm.)
    Collection Lisbeth Bissier, Ascona
21. Mohnkolben 2 1938. 1938.
    24⅝ x 18⅞" (62.5 x 48 cm.)
    Collection Lisbeth Bissier, Ascona
22. Schote 1939. 1939.
    24⅜ x 18⅞" (62 x 48 cm.)
23. 1940 Blütenentfaltung III. 1940.
    24¾ x 18⅛" (63 x 46.5 cm.)
24. 1948 E. 1948.
    18¾ x 24¼" (47.5 x 61.5 cm.)
    Collection Lisbeth Bissier, Ascona
25. 48 Zwei Formen. 1948.
    18¾ x 24⅜" (47.6 x 62 cm.)
26. 4.10.48 Viereck und Dreieck. 1948.
    18⅞ x 24¾" (48 x 63 cm.)
    Collection Lisbeth Bissier, Ascona
27. 1949 zwei Divergierende. 1949.
    18¾ x 24¾" (47.7 x 63 cm.)
    Collection Lisbeth Bissier, Ascona
28. Muschel 49. 1949.
    19 x 24¾" (48.2 x 62.7 cm.)
29. 19.4.58. 1958.
    15½ x 20⅝" (39.5 x 52.3 cm.)
    Collection Lisbeth Bissier, Ascona
30. 26.febr.59 y. 1959.
    15½ x 20⅝" (39.5 x 52.5 cm.)
31. 13.5.59 M. 1959.
    19⅛ x 24⅝" (48.5 x 62.5 cm.)
32. G I.59.9. 1959.
    15½ x 20⅝" (39.5 x 52.5 cm.)
33. 14.Sept.59 AH. 1959.
    19⅛ x 24⅝" (48.7 x 62.7 cm.)
34. 16.9.59 G. 1959.
    19⅛ x 24⅝" (48.6 x 62.5 cm.)
35. 4.4.60.XI. 1960.
    15½ x 20⅝" (39.5 x 52.5 cm.)
    Lent by Galerie Beyeler, Basel
36. 18.II.61 Wu. 1961.
    15½ x 20¾" (39.3 x 52.6 cm.)
37. 18.febr.61 d. 1961.
    15½ x 20⅝" (39.2 x 52.5 cm.)
38. 28.4.61.8. 1961.
    15⅛ x 20⅝" (38.5 x 52.2 cm.)
39. H 4.März 64. 1964.
    19⅛ x 24½" (48.5 x 62.2 cm.)
40. 17.3.64. 1964.
    19⅛ x 24⅝" (48.5 x 62.5 cm.)
    Collection Lisbeth Bissier, Ascona

MONOTYPES, OIL ON PAPER

41. 48 (18). 1948.
    19¼ x 25¼″ (49 x 64 cm.)
42. 23.9.50 I. 1950.
    31⅝ x 39¼″ (80.3 x 99.6 cm.)
43. 6.5.51. 1951.
    38½ x 32⅛″ (97.7 x 81.6 cm.)
44. 5.7.51 II. 1951.
    29 x 33⅝″ (73.5 x 85.5 cm.)
45. 10.12.51. 1951.
    39¾ x 33⅝″ (101 x 85.5 cm.)
46. 29.III.52. 1952.
    40⅛ x 28¾″ (102 x 73 cm.)
47. 24.II.52. Rotes Gehäuse bedroht
    mit eisenfarbenem Pfeil. 1952.
    40 x 29″ (101.5 x 73.5 cm.)
48. 3.XI.52 I. 1952.
    40⅛ x 28⅞″ (102 x 73.4 cm.)

WOODCUTS, INK ON PAPER

49. 49 II/6. 1949.
    18⅞ x 24¾″ (48 x 63 cm.)
50. ca.50 Platte II/3a. 1950.
    24¾ x 18⅞″ (62.8 x 48 cm.)
51. 10.2.51. 1951.
    19⅛ x 24¾″ (48.5 x 62.8 cm.)

52. 1953. 1953. Collection Lisbeth Bissier, Ascona.

WATERCOLORS, ON PAPER

52. 1953. 1953.
9⅛ x 8⅝″ (23.3 x 22 cm.)
Collection Lisbeth Bissier, Ascona

53. 25.11.56. 1956.
7⅝ x 9⅞″ (19.5 x 25 cm.)

54. Tourettes 2.6.57 schg. 1957.
6¾ x 9⅝″ (17.3 x 24.4 cm.)
Collection Lisbeth Bissier, Ascona

55. Ascona 5.X.58. 1958.
6¼ x 9⅝″ (16 x 24.5 cm.)

56. 22.August 59. 1959.
6 x 9¼″ (15.2 x 23.5 cm.)

57. deo gratias Ronco 18.X.59 N. 1959.
6 x 9½″ (15.2 x 24.2 cm.)

58. 7.Febr.60 Athos. 1960.
6½ x 10″ (16.5 x 25.4 cm.)
Joseph H. Hirshhorn Collection, New York

59. 2.August 60. 1960.
6¼ x 9¼″ (15.9 x 23.5 cm.)
Collection Mr. and Mrs. David Steine, Nashville

60. 22.Mai 61. 1961.
5½ x 9½″ (14 x 24.2 cm.)
Joseph H. Hirshhorn Collection, New York

61. 27.6.61. 1961.
6⅝ x 9⅝″ (16.9 x 24.5 cm.)

62. 5.Nov.61 Rondine. 1961.
6¼ x 9½″ (15.8 x 24.2 cm.)
Collection Lisbeth Bissier, Ascona

63. a.26.Juli 62. 1962.
7⅝ x 9⅝″ (19.3 x 24.4 cm.)
Collection Lisbeth Bissier, Ascona

64. Mori bundus Sal. A 18.oct 62. 1962.
10 x 12″ (25.4 x 30.5 cm.)
Collection Mrs. John Lefebre, New York

65. A.22.10.62. 1962.
9⅝ x 12⅜″ (24.3 x 31.4 cm.)

66. A.21.Jan.63. 1963.
6⅜ x 9½″ (16.2 x 24 cm.)
Collection Lisbeth Bissier, Ascona

67. △.26.6.63. 1963.
9⅝ x 12¼″ (24.3 x 31 cm.)

68. 12.Jan.64 M. 1964.
7⅞ x 9⅝″ (19.9 x 24.4 cm.)

69. 28.1.65 qu. 1965.
9½ x 11⅜″ (24 x 29 cm.)

70. 29.Jan.65. 1965.
9¾ x 12⅝″ (24.6 x 32 cm.)

71. 24.Febr.65. 1965.
9⅝ x 12¼″ (24.3 x 31 cm.)

72. 30.März 65. 1965.
6⅞ x 9⅛″ (17.3 x 23 cm.)
Collection Lisbeth Bissier, Ascona

58. 7.Febr.60 Athos. 1960. Joseph H. Hirshhorn Collection, New York.

SMALL-FORMAT EGG-OIL TEMPERAS, ON CANVAS

73. 14.III.56. 1956.
    7 x 7¼″ (17.7 x 18.3 cm.)
74. 23.X.56. Ascona MN. 1956.
    9½ x 9⅛″ (24 x 23 cm.)
    Collection Lisbeth Bissier, Ascona
75. 9.I.57. 1957.
    5⅛ x 7⅛″ (13 x 18 cm.)
76. 18.5.57. 1957.
    7½ x 9⅛″ (19 x 23 cm.)
    Collection Staatliche Museen Preussischer
    Kulturbesitz,
    Nationalgalerie, Berlin
    (shown in Pittsburgh, Dallas and New York only)

77. 24.Sept.57. [egg-oil tempera on pongee silk] 1957.
    5⅞ x 7⅜″ (15 x 18.6 cm.)
78. 21.10.57. 1957.
    7½ x 8¼″ (19 x 21 cm.)
    Collection Lisbeth Bissier, Ascona
79. Ronco 23.Mai 58. 1958.
    8¼ x 11″ (21 x 28 cm.)
    Collection Dr. Werner Schmalenbach, Düsseldorf
80. Ronco 27.5.58. 1958.
    5 x 9⅝″ (12.8 x 24.5 cm.)
81. 31.Juli 58. 1958.
    8 x 8½″ (20.3 x 21.6 cm.)
    Collection Mr. and Mrs. Peter A. Silverman, Toronto
82. 25.Nov.58. 1958.
    7⅜ x 10¼″ (18.7 x 25.9 cm.)

64. Mori bundus Sal. A 18.oct 62. 1962. Collection Mrs. John Lefebre, New York.

83. 18.Dez.58 A. 1958.
9 x 9⅞″ (22.9 x 25.1 cm.)
Lent by Lefebre Gallery, New York

84. 20.Jan.59. 1959.
7⅞ x 9¼″ (20 x 23.5 cm.)
Collection The Trustees of the Tate Gallery, London

85. 18.Febr.59.M. 1959.
7¾ x 8½″ (19.5 x 21.5 cm.) *sight dimension*
Collection Erhart and Anita Kästner, Wolfenbüttel

86. 29.III.59. 1959.
7⅜ x 9⅛″ (18.7 x 23 cm.)
Lent by Lefebre Gallery, New York

87. Es hat sich zum Leben entschieden Ronco 23.
April 59. 1959.
7¼ x 9⅛″ (18.3 x 23 cm.)
Collection Lisbeth Bissier, Ascona

88. 8.Juni 59. Missa in festes. 1959.
7⅝ x 11⅝″ (19.5 x 29.5 cm.)
Collection Lisbeth Bissier, Ascona

89. 6.Juli 59. 1959.
8¼ x 11¼″ (21 x 28.6 cm.)
Collection The Museum of Modern Art, New York
Gertrud A. Mellon Fund

90. 19 Juli 59. Yin Yang. 1959.
7½ x 9⅛″ (19 x 23.2 cm.)
Collection Mrs. Andrew Fuller, New York

91. 5. 6. Aug.59. 1959.
6⅞ x 9½″ (17.5 x 24.2 cm.)

92. 9.August 59 Ko. 1959.
7⅝ x 9¼″ (19.5 x 23.5 cm.)

93. 14.September 59 Mona. 1959.
7⅜ x 9⅝″ (18.7 x 24.3 cm.)
Collection Lisbeth Bissier, Ascona

94. 3.März 60 Lass es ges. 1960.
8 x 9¼″ (20.3 x 23.5 cm.)
Collection New England Merchants National Bank
of Boston

95. 4 April 60. H. 1960.
7¼ x 9¼″ (18.4 x 23.5 cm.)
Collection Mr. and Mrs. Peter A. Silverman, Toronto

96. 16.April 1960. 1960.
8⅜ x 9⅝″ (21.3 x 24.3 cm.)

97. 21.April 60 Y. 1960.
7⅛ x 10″ (18.1 x 25.5 cm.)
Collection Lisbeth Bissier, Ascona

98. 11 August 60 drei Kreuze. 1960.
6¾ x 8⅞″ (17.2 x 22.6 cm.)
Contemporary Collection of
The Cleveland Museum of Art

99. 14 August 60 K. 1960.
7½ x 8⅝″ (19 x 21.9 cm.)
Collection Marion Lefebre, New York

100. 19.Sept.60 K. 1960.
6¼ x 8⅞″ (16 x 22.5 cm.)

101. 10.Nov.60. Eloh. 1960.
5⅜ x 8¾″ (13.6 x 22.2 cm.)

102. Monti 60.58 Cista. 1960.
7⅝ x 8¾″ (19.2 x 22.2 cm.)

103. 5.März 61. 1961.
8¼ x 9¾″ (21 x 24.8 cm.)
Collection Marion Lefebre, New York

104. 10.April 61 M. 1961.
7⅛ x 8½″ (18.1 x 21.6 cm.)
Collection Sarah G. Austin, New York

105. 18.April 61. 1961.
8½ x 10½″ (21.6 x 26.7 cm.) *sight dimension*
Collection Mrs. H. Gates Lloyd, Haverford,
Pennsylvania

106. 4.6.61 A. 1961.
8½ x 10⅜″ (21.6 x 26.3 cm.)
Collection John Lefebre, New York

107. 16.6.61 K. 1961.
5½ x 9¼″ (14 x 23.5 cm.)
Collection Mr. and Mrs. R. B. Schulhof, New York

108. 4 Oct 61 K. 1961.
7¼ x 8¾″ (18.4 x 22.2 cm.)
Collection Mr. and Mrs. Gustave Levy, New York

109. 7 Oct 61 Jean. 1961.
7¾ x 8¼″ (19.7 x 21 cm.)
Collection Mr. and Mrs. George Labalme, Jr.,
New York

110. Serodine 61 10.10. 1961.
    8 x 8½" (20.3 x 21.6 cm.) *sight dimension*
    Collection Mrs. Robert M. Benjamin, New York
111. Rondine 18.X.61. 1961.
    7¼ x 8½" (18.4 x 21.6 cm.) .
    Collection Mr. and Mrs. Gustave Levy, New York
112. Rondine 3.Nov.61 Mi. 1961.
    6⅛ x 9⅞" (15.5 x 25 cm.)
    Collection Lisbeth Bissier, Ascona
113. 2.febr. 62 A. 1962.
    7¾ x 9⅞" (19.5 x 25 cm.)
114. Ascona 22.febr.62. 1962.
    5 x 9½" (12.7 x 24.1 cm.)
    Collection Mr. and Mrs. Richard Hofstadter, New York
115. 26.März 62 K. 1962.
    7⅞ x 8⅝" (20 x 21.8 cm.)
116. A 24.6.62. 1962.
    5¼ x 9½" (13.3 x 24 cm.) *sight dimension*
    Collection Mrs. Robert M. Benjamin, New York
117. A 3.Juli 62. 1962.
    7⅛ x 8⅞" (18 x 22.5 cm.)
118. 10.11.62 B Gamma. 1962.
    6¼ x 9½" (16 x 24 cm.)
119. Wann etwa? A. 4.3.63. 1963.
    5½ x 9½" (13.8 x 24 cm.)

120. H. 12.Mai 63. 1963.
    5⅛ x 8¾" (13 x 22.3 cm.)
121. Δ.25.8.63. 1963.
    6¾ x 9⅝" (17 x 24.5 cm.)
122. A 18.oct.63. 1963.
    7⅜ x 10⅝" (18.8 x 26.8 cm.)
123. 8.febr.64. 1964.
    8⅛ x 9¾" (20.6 x 24.7 cm.)
124. 20.febr.64 qu. 1964.
    7⅜ x 9⅞" (18.8 x 25 cm.)
125. 13.März 65 Z. 1965.
    8⅛ x 12⅜" (20.7 x 31.5 cm.)
    Collection Lisbeth Bissier, Ascona
126. 4.April 65.R. 1965.
    5½ x 9⅞" (14.1 x 25 cm.)
127. 7.April 65. 1965.
    8⅝ x 14¾" (22 x 37.3 cm.)
128. 8.April 65. No. 1965.
    7⅞ x 10⅜" (20.1 x 26.3 cm.)
129. 29.April 65. 1965.
    7⅛ x 11⅞" (18 x 30.2 cm.)
130. H. 17.Mai 65. 1965.
    8⅞ x 11⅜" (22.5 x 29 cm.)
131. 8.Juni Nop 65. 1965.
    7⅝ x 8⅜" (19.3 x 21.3 cm.)

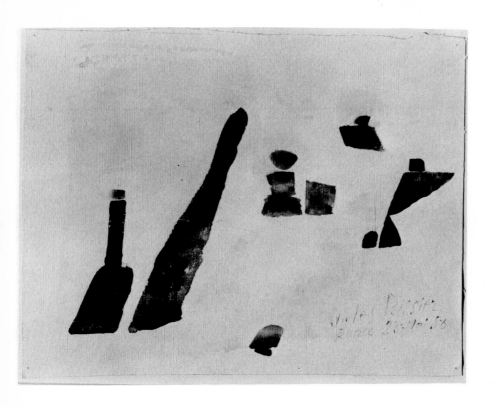

79. Ronco 23.Mai 58. 1958. Collection Dr. Werner Schmalenbach, Düsseldorf.

LARGE-FORMAT EGG-OIL TEMPERAS, ON CANVAS

132. 24.Sept.60 Pa. 1960.
    16⅛ x 19″ (41 x 48.3 cm.)

133. 4.Dez.60. 1960.
    17⅜ x 21⅞″ (44 x 55.6 cm.)
    Collection Staatliche Museen Preussischer
    Kulturbesitz, Nationalgalerie, Berlin
    (shown in Pittsburgh, Dallas and New York only)

134. 5.Mai 60 + 7.Februar 61. 1961.
    17⅝ x 21⅛″ (44.7 x 53. 8 cm.)
    Collection Lisbeth Bissier, Ascona

135. Dunkler Pfingsttag 61. 1961.
    19 x 20″ (48.2 x 50.8 cm.)
    Collection Mr. and Mrs. L. F. Gittler, New York

136. 1.Juni 61. 1961.
    16½ x 22½″ (42 x 57 cm.)
    Collection Staatsgalerie, Stuttgart

137. 21.Juli 61 ogta Zwillinge. 1961.
    16⅞ x 18¼″ (43 x 46.2 cm.)
    Collection Lisbeth Bissier, Ascona

138. 25.Juli 61. 1961.
    17⅛ x 19⅞″ (43.5 x 50.5 cm.)

139. Rondine 18.Dez.61. 1961.
    17⅜ x 19⅝″ (44.2 x 49.8 cm.)

140. 24.12.61 Rondine CMB. 1961.
    17¾ x 22¾″ (45 x 57.8 cm.)

141. 14.febr.62 Rondine. 1962.
    17⅛ x 22½″ (43.6 x 57 cm.)

142. A.15.Dez.62. 1962.
    17½ x 21⅞″ (44.5 x 55.4 cm.)
    Collection Lisbeth Bissier, Ascona

143. △.3.April 63. 1963.
    17⅞ x 22″ (45.5 x 56 cm.)
    Collection Lisbeth Bissier, Ascona

144. pro memoria di Giacomo 30 Nov 63. 1963.
    15½ x 20″ (39.4 x 50.8 cm.)
    Collection Mr. and Mrs. Jerome Brody, New York

145. A.5.April 64. 1964.
    15½ x 19½″ (39.4 x 49.5 cm.)
    Collection Museum of Fine Arts, Boston.
    Sophie M. Friedman Fund

146. △.18.Mai 64. 1964.
    17⅜ x 21⅛″ (44.2 x 53.6 cm.)

147. A.4.Juni 64. 1964.
    17¾ x 23″ (45 x 58.3 cm.)
    Collection Lisbeth Bissier, Ascona

148. a.6.Juni 64. 1964.
    15⅜ x 19¾″ (39 x 50 cm.)

149. 24.7.64. 1964.
    17¾ x 22⅞″ (45 x 58 cm.)
    Collection Lisbeth Bissier, Ascona

150. 12.März 65. 1965.
    17⅛ x 21⅝″ (43.5 x 54.8 cm.)

151. 18.März 65. 1965.
    17⅛ x 21¼″ (43.5 x 54 cm.)
    Collection Lisbeth Bissier, Ascona

152. 12.April 65. 1965.
    15⅝ x 20⅜″ (39.6 x 51.8 cm.)
    Collection Lisbeth Bissier, Ascona

81. 31.Juli 58. 1958. Collection Mr. and Mrs. Peter A. Silverman, Toronto.

KUNSTVEREIN, Freiburg-im-Breisgau, Germany, 1920.

KUNSTHAUS, Zürich, 1923, and KUNSTGALERIE LUD-WIG SCHAMES, Frankfurt am Main, Germany, 1923.

AUGUSTREUM, Oldenburg, Germany, 1929.

GALERIE HERMANN, Stuttgart, Germany, 1947.

GALERIE RUHSTRAT, Hamburg, Germany, 1950.

ZIMMERGALERIE FRANK, Frankfurt am Main, 1951.

STUDIO FÜR MODERNE KUNST, Wuppertal, Germany, 1952.

KUNSTVEREIN, Freiburg-im-Breisgau, 1952 (with Max Bill and Vantongerloo).

GALERIE PROBST, Mannheim, Germany, 1953.

GALERIE DU THÉÂTRE CENTRAL, Zürich, September 26—October 22, 1953.
Review: Werk, Winterthur, vol. 40, no. 11, November 1953, p. 200 (supp.).

KUNSTVEREIN, Freiburg-im-Breisgau, July 1954.
Catalogue published: introduction by Siegfried E. Bröse.

SCHLOSS ARBON, Arbon, Switzerland, September 1956 (with Hans Arp).

ZIMMERGALERIE FRANK, Frankfurt am Main, 1956.
Review: Thwaites, J. A., "On Exhibit in Germany", *Pictures on Exhibit,* New York, vol. 20, no. 3, December 1956, p. 51.

KUNSTVEREIN, Freiburg-im-Breisgau, June 1958 (with Jurg Spiller).

KESTNER-GESELLSCHAFT, Hannover, Germany, October 24—November 30, 1958.
Exhibition traveled in Germany to: KUNSTHALLE, Bremen; ULMER MUSEUM, Ulm; STADTISCHES MUSEUM, Duisburg; KARL-ERNST-OSTHAUS-MUSEUM, Hagen.
Catalogue published: introduction by Werner Schmalenbach; bibliographical data; illus.: 18 black and white; checklist of 180 works.
Review: Bayl, Friederich, "Präkolumbisch, Dada, Bissier, Platscheck", *Art International,* Zürich, vol. 2, no. 9/10, 1958, pp. 84, 102.

GALERIE ST. STEPHEN, Vienna, May 1-16, 1959.

GALERIE CHARLES LIENHARD, Zürich, October 7-November 7, 1959.
Catalogue published: introduction by Werner Schmalenbach; bibliographical data; illus.: 2 black and white, 5 color; checklist of 163 works.
Review: Werk, Winterthur, vol. 46, no. 12, December 1959, p. 262 (supp.).

GEMEENTEMUSEUM, The Hague, The Netherlands, November 7, 1959-January 3, 1960.
Catalogue published: introduction by Werner Schmalenbach; bibliographical data; illus.: 19 black and white; checklist of 131 works.

GIMPEL FILS, London, May 24-June 18, 1960.
Catalogue published: introduction by Werner Schmalenbach.
Review: Mock, J. Y., "Sandra Blow and Bissier at the Gimpel Gallery", *Apollo,* London, vol. 71, no. 424, June 1960, p. 193.

XXX BIENNALE, Venice, German Pavilion (separate gallery), June-October 1960. *General catalogue for Biennale published:* Introduced to German section by Hans Konrad Röthel; checklist of 40 works, p. 230.

GALERIE DANIEL CORDIER, Paris, October 6-November 5, 1960.
Catalogue published: introduction by Marcel Brion; bibliographical data; illus.: 11 black and white; checklist of 168 works.
Review: Aujourd'hui, Boulogne, vol. 5, no. 29, December 1960, p. 49.

PALAIS DES BEAUX-ARTS, Brussels, February 11-March 5, 1961.
Catalogue published: introduction by Will Grohmann; biography; illus.: 11 black and white; checklist of 102 works.

BEZALEL NATIONAL ART MUSEUM, Jerusalem, May 20-June 21, 1961.
Catalogue published: illus.: 4 black and white; checklist of 40 works.

VI BIENAL DE SÃO PAULO, São Paulo, Brazil, German Section (separate gallery), September-December 1961. *General catalogue for Bienal published:* introduction to German section by Werner Schmalenbach, pp. 109-111; checklist of 72 works, pp. 114-116.

LEFEBRE GALLERY, New York, November 7-December 2, 1961.

Catalogue published: introduction by Werner Schmalenbach; bibliographical data; illus.: 2 black and white, 1 color.

Reviews: Art News, New York, vol. 60, no. 8, December 1961, p. 56; Raynor, V., "Exhibition at Lefebre Gallery", *Arts,* New York, vol. 36, no. 4, January 1962, p. 35.

MUSEU DE ARTE MODERNA, Rio de Janeiro, Brazil, 1962.

THE PARK LANE, Buffalo, New York, January 14-February 10, 1962 (with Paul Klee).

Catalogue published: checklist of 7 works.

GALERIE BEYELER, Basel, Switzerland, April 1-30, 1962.

Catalogue published: statements by Julius Bissier; bibliographical data; illus.: 10 black and white, 7 color; checklist of 87 works.

WORLD HOUSE GALLERIES, New York, April 24-May 12, 1962 (with Roger Bissière).

Catalogue published: illus.: 1 black and white; checklist of 8 works.

Review: Art News, New York, vol. 61, no. 4, Summer 1962, p. 49.

GALERIE STANGL, Munich, Germany, May 29-July 7, 1962.

Catalogue published: statements by Julius Bissier; bibliographical data; illus.: 16 black and white.

Review: Roh, J., "Kunstbrief aus München", *Das Kunstwerk,* Baden-Baden, vol. 16, no. 4, October 1962, p. 15.

KUNSTVEREIN, Hamburg, August 24-September 23, 1962; Exhibition traveled in Germany to: ULMER MUSEUM, Ulm, October 7-November 4, 1962; STAATSGALERIE, Stuttgart, November 25-December 30, 1962; VON DER HEYDT MUSEUM, Wuppertal, January 13-February 24, 1963; KUNSTHALLE, Mannheim, March 8-April 15, 1963; AUGUSTINERMUSEUM, Freiburg-im-Breisgau, May 5-June 9, 1963.

Catalogue published: introduction by Herbert Pée; bibliographical data; illus.: 16 black and white, 8 color; checklist of 110 works.

LEFEBRE GALLERY, New York, February 26-March 30, 1963.

Catalogue published: introduction by John Lefebre; bibliographical data; illus.: 13 black and white.

Review: Art News, New York, vol. 62, no. 2, April 1963, pp. 10-11.

GIMPEL FILS, London, May 21-June 18, 1963.

Catalogue published: bibliographical data; illus.: 14 black and white, 1 color; checklist of 75 works.

Review: Gordon, Alastair, "Exhibition at Gimpel Fils", *Connoisseur,* London, vol. 153, no. 616, June 1963, p. 153.

KUNSTMUSEUM, St. Gallen, Switzerland, June 16-August 15, 1963 (with Arp, Nicholson, Tobey and Valenti).

Review: Werk, Winterthur, vol. 50, no. 8, August 1963, p. 181 (supp.).

GALERIE BEYELER, Basel, October 15-December 31, 1963 (with Arp, Nicholson and Tobey).

Review: Werk, Winterthur, vol. 50, no. 12, December 1963, p. 267 (supp.).

INSTITUTE OF CONTEMPORARY ART, Boston, November 1-December 8, 1963. Exhibition traveled in the United States to: THE ARTS CLUB OF CHICAGO, Chicago, December 21, 1963-January 18, 1964; THE DETROIT INSTITUTE OF ARTS, Detroit, February 10-March 23, 1964; MUNSON-WILLIAMS-PROCTOR INSTITUTE, Utica, New York, April 19-May 31, 1964; U.C.L.A. ART GALLERIES, Los Angeles, June 21-July 31, 1964.

Catalogue published: introduction by Sue M. Thurman; bibliographical data; illus.: 12 black and white, 9 color; checklist of 130 works.

Review: Rigelhaupt, Eleanor, "Shock treatment for Boston ", *Art in America,* New York, vol. 51, no. 2, April 1963, p. 134.

GALERIE STANGL, Munich, May 14-June 30, 1964.

Catalogue published: illus.: 12 black and white, 3 color.

PAULA JOHNSON GALLERY, New York, October 13-31, 1964.

Reviews: Art News, New York, vol. 63, no. 8, December 1964, p. 13; Tillim, Sidney, "Exhibition at Johnson Gallery", *Arts,* New York, vol. 39, no. 3, December 1964, p. 70.

GALERIA LA MEDUSA, Rome, September 1964.

Catalogue published: bibliographical data; illus.: 4 black and white, 1 color.

Review: Art International, Lugano, vol. 8, no. 8, October 1964, p. 48.

LEFEBRE GALLERY, New York, February 9-March 6, 1965. Traveled to: FORT WORTH ART CENTER, Fort Worth, Texas, March 1965.

Catalogue published: introduction by Erhart Kästner; bibliographical data; illus.: 9 black and white, 1 color.

Reviews: Art News, New York, vol. 64, no. 1, March 1965, p. 13; Stiles, G., "Exhibition at Lefebre Gallery", *Arts,* vol. 39, no. 7, April 1965, p. 58.

R. N. KETTERER, Campione, Switzerland, March 1-31, 1965.

Catalogue published: illus.: 42 black and white; checklist of 42 works.

AMERICAN ART GALLERY, Copenhagen, March 30-April 24, 1965.

Catalogue published: bibliographical data; illus.: 8 black and white; checklist of 21 works.

SCOTTISH NATIONAL GALLERY OF MODERN ART, Edinburgh, July 31-September 19, 1965.

Catalogue published: introduction by Douglas Hall; bibliographical data; illus.: 4 black and white; checklist of 30 works.

Review: Irwin, D., "Edinburgh Festival", *Burlington Magazine,* vol. 107, no. 751, October 1965, p. 540.

TONINELLI ARTE MODERNA, Milan, February-March 1966.

Catalogue published: introduction by Werner Schmalenbach; bibliographical data; illus.: 10 black and white, 5 color; checklist of 34 works.

GALLERIA LA BUSSOLA, Turin, Italy, 1966.

GIMPEL & HANOVER GALERIE, Zürich, April 29-May 28, 1966.

Catalogue published: short biography; illus.: 6 black and white; checklist of 34 works.

Review: Werk, Winterthur, vol. 53, no. 6, June 1966, p. 140 (supp.).

ULMER MUSEUM, Ulm, Germany, 1966 (tapestries).

GALERIE ALICE PAULI, Lausanne, Switzerland, June 4-July 23, 1966.

Catalogue published: introduction by Andre Kuenzi; bibliographical data; illus.: 10 black and white; checklist of 51 works.

LEFEBRE GALLERY, New York, "Drawings and Brushdrawings 1935-1964", October 16-28; "Monotypes", November 1-26; "Miniatures", November 29-December 24, 1966.

Catalogue published: introduction by Werner Schmalenbach; bibliographical data; illus.: 7 black and white, 2 color.

Reviews: Art News, New York, vol. 65, no. 7, November 1966, p. 10; *Art News,* New York, vol. 65, no. 8, December 1966, p. 8.

GALERIE STANGL, Munich, June 21-July 31, 1967.

Catalogue published: bibliographical data; illus.: 15 black and white; checklist of 78 works.

KUNSTMUSEUM, Winterthur, Switzerland, October 8-November 12, 1967, and AARGAUER KUNSTHAUS, Aarau, Switzerland, January 10-February 25, 1968.

Catalogue published: introduction by Manuel Gasser; bibliographical data; illus.: 16 black and white, 3 color; checklist of 162 works.

XXIX BIENNALE, Venice, German Pavilion, June-October 1958 (8 works).

II. DOCUMENTA '59, Kassel, "Kunst nach 1954", July 11-October 11, 1959 (9 works).

CARNEGIE INSTITUTE (Department of Fine Arts), Pittsburgh, "The 1961 Pittsburgh International Exhibition of Contemporary Painting and Sculpture", October 27, 1961-January 7, 1962 (6 works).

WORLD'S FAIR, Seattle, "Art Since 1950: American and International", April 21-October 21, 1962 (5 works).

DOCUMENTA III, Kassel, June 27-October 5, 1964 (18 works).

MUSEUM OF ART, CARNEGIE INSTITUTE, Pittsburgh, "The 1964 Pittsburgh International Exhibition of Contemporary Painting and Sculpture", October 30, 1964-January 10, 1965 (6 works).

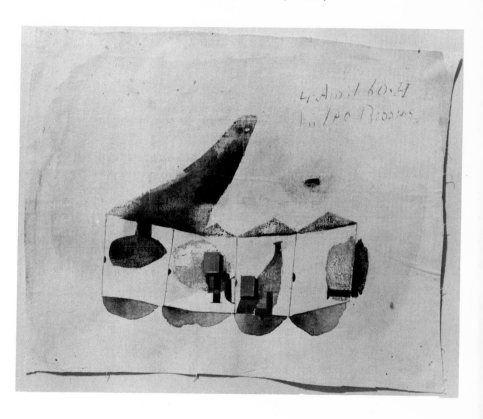

95. 4 April 60. H. 1960. Collection Mr. and Mrs. Peter A. Silverman, Toronto.

SELECTED BIBLIOGRAPHY   BOOKS

Catalogue monographs are listed in the exhibition section under the publishing institution.

LEONHARD, KURT. *Julius Bissier,* Stuttgart, KG-Verlag, 1947.

LEONHARD, KURT. *Augenschein und Inbegriff,* Stuttgart, Deutsche Verlagsanstalt, 1953.

BRION, MARCEL. *Art Abstrait,* Paris, Editions Albin Michel, 1956, pp. 265-266.

SEUPHOR, MICHEL. *Dictionary of Abstract Painting,* translated by Lionel Izod, John Montague and Francis Scarfe, New York, Tudor Publishing Company, 1957, pp. 72, 134.

GROHMANN, WILL. "Germany, Austria, Switzerland", in *Art Since 1945,* edited by Milton S. Fox, New York, Harry N. Abrams, Inc., 1958, p. 174.

PONENTE, NELLO. *Modern Painting, Contemporary Trends,* translated by James Emmons, New York, Skira, 1960, pp. 94, 184.

SCHMALENBACH, WERNER, *Julius Bissier, Farbige Miniaturen,* Munich, R. Piper & Co. Verlag, 1960.

KÄSTNER, ERHART, "Für Julius Bissier", *Jahresring 62/63,* Stuttgart, Deutsche Verlagsanstalt, 1963.

SCHMALENBACH, WERNER. *Bissier.* Stuttgart, Verlag Gert Hatje, 1963; English edition: New York, Harry N. Abrams, Inc., 1963.

KÄSTNER, ERHART. "An Julius Bissier", *Die Lerchenschule,* Frankfurt a.M., Insel-Verlag, 1964.

HAFTMANN, WERNER. *Painting in the Twentieth Century,* New York, Frederick A. Praeger, Inc., 1965, pp. 369-370, 382.

VALLIER, DORA. *Julius Bissier, Tuschen 1934-1964,* Stuttgart, Verlag Gert Hatje, 1965; English edition: New York, Lefebre Gallery, 1965.

ROH, FRANZ. "Bissier", in *Les Peintres Contemporains,* Paris, Editions Lucien Mezenod, 1965, pp. 160-163.

GROHMANN, WILL. "Germany, Austria, and Switzerland", in *New Art Around the World, Painting and Sculpture,* New York, Harry N. Abrams, Inc., 1966, pp. 294-295.

PELLEGRINI, ALDO. *New Tendencies in Art,* translated by Robin Carson, New York, Crown Publishers, Inc., 1966, pp. 44-45.

ZEHM, FREDERICH. *Lyrische Kantate nach 6 Gedichten von Julius Bissier,* Mainz, Schott-Verlag, 1967.

PERIODICALS

VIETTA, EGON. "Julius Bissier", *Das Kunstwerk*, Baden-Baden, vol. 3, no. 8/9, 1950, pp. 52-54.

BRÖSE, S. E. "Die Tuschen des Julius Bissier", *Das Bilderhaus*, Kunstverein, Freiburg-im-Breisgau, no. 8, 1955.

BAYL, FRIEDERICH. "Zur XXIX Biennale", *Art International*, Zürich, vol. 2, no. 6/7, 1958, pp. 39-40, 49.

SCHMALENBACH, WERNER. "Julius Bissier", *Die Kunst und Das Schöne Heim*, Munich, vol. 57, no. 8, May 1959, pp. 288-291.

SCHMALENBACH, WERNER. "Julius Bissier", *Quadrum 7*, Brussels, 1959, pp. 63-74.

ALLOWAY, LAWRENCE. "Venice-Europe 1960", *Art International*, Zürich, vol. 4, no. 7, September 25, 1960, pp. 27, 46.

GROHMANN, WILL. "Der Staat als Mazen: Kunst an den Freiburger Universitätsbauten", *Quadrum 9*, Brussels, 1960, pp. 26-27, 192.

RESTANY, PIERRE. "Julius Bissier", *Cimaise*, Paris, vol. 7, no. 6, January-February 1961, pp. 12-25.

SCHIFF, GERT. "The VI São Paulo Bienal", *Art International*, Zürich, vol. 5, no. 10, Christmas 1961, pp. 55, 60-61.

————————————— . *Time Magazine*, New York, November 8, 1963, pp. 70-71.

GASSER, MANUEL. "Julius Bissier", *Du*, Zürich, vol. 23, August, 1963, pp. 13-24.

MAHLOW, DIETRICH. "Warum geschriebene Bilder?", *Das Kunstwerk*, Baden-Baden, vol. 16, no. 10, April 1963, pp. 2-3, 10.

HENNING, EDWARD B. "In pursuit of content; works of contemporary art acquired during the past two years", *The Bulletin of The Cleveland Museum of Art*, Cleveland, vol. 50, no. 8, October 1963, pp. 225-226.

THURMAN, SUE M. "Julius Bissier", *Art International*, Lugano, vol. 8, no. 1, February 15, 1964, pp. 21-24 and cover illus. (reprint of introduction to the exhibition catalogue, Institute of Contemporary Art, Boston, 1963).

HODIN, J. P. "Quand les artistes parlent du sacre", *XXe Siècle*, Paris, no. 24, December 1964, p. 19.

LEFEBRE, JOHN. "Julius Bissier", *Das Kunstwerk*, Baden-Baden, vol. 18, no. 6, December 1964, pp. 4-11 and cover illus.

Mrs. Lisbeth Bissier, Ascona, courteously supplied all but
the following photographs, which were taken by:

Contemporary Collection of The Cleveland Museum of Art, no. 98
Paul Katz, New York, nos. 58, 135
Walter Klein, Düsseldorf, no. 79
Robert E. Mates, New York, no. 116
O. E. Nelson, New York, nos. 64, 99
San Francisco Museum of Art, nos. 81, 95

152. 12.April 65. 1965. Collection Lisbeth Bissier, Ascona.

PARTICIPATING INSTITUTIONS SAN FRANCISCO MUSEUM OF ART

THE PHILLIPS COLLECTION, WASHINGTON, D.C.

CARNEGIE INSTITUTE MUSEUM OF ART, PITTSBURGH

DALLAS MUSEUM OF FINE ARTS

THE SOLOMON R. GUGGENHEIM MUSEUM, NEW YORK

3000 copies of this catalogue,
designed by Arthur S. Congdon,
have been printed by Sterlip Press, New York,
in September 1968
on the occasion of the loan exhibition
"Julius Bissier (1893-1965): A Retrospective Exhibition."